Seasons:

The Stages of Life

By Dr. Alfie Wines

IN MEMORY OF:

My Beloved Parents
Alphonso and Nellie Beth Hart Terry

With Love and Gratitude to:
Tajiri Brackens, Beloved Daughter

My Brother and his wife, Anthony and Linda Terry

My Nephew and his wife, Anthony DeShon and LaToya Terry
Their children Brittiny and Anthony Charles Terry

My Nieces: Beth, Tamika, and Tanisha Terry

Johnrice Newton who invited me to Union Cathedral Women's Conference, A Woman of All Seasons
Anatole Hotel, Dallas TX, November 10, 2011
for which the "Seasons" concept was birthed and presented

Rev. Cynthia Cole – Encourager Par Excellence

Dr. Stacey-Floyd Thomas – Professor and Mentor Par Excellence

All of the family, friends, professors, and colleagues
who encouraged me along the way

TABLE OF CONTENTS

"Turn! Turn! Turn!"

To everything - turn, turn, turn
There is a season - turn, turn, turn
And a time to every purpose under heaven

A time to be born, a time to die
A time to plant, a time to reap
A time to kill, a time to heal
A time to laugh, a time to weep

To everything - turn, turn, turn
There is a season - turn, turn, turn
And a time to every purpose under heaven

A time to build up, a time to break down
A time to dance, a time to mourn
A time to cast away stones
A time to gather stones together

To everything - turn, turn, turn
There is a season - turn, turn, turn
And a time to every purpose under heaven

A time of love, a time of hate
A time of war, a time of peace
A time you may embrace
A time to refrain from embracing

To everything - turn, turn, turn
There is a season - turn, turn, turn
And a time to every purpose under heaven

A time to gain, a time to lose
A time to rend, a time to sew
A time for love, a time for hate
A time for peace, I swear it's not too late!

1

Introduction

I don't know how many times I listened to the 60's classic, "Turn, Turn, Turn" before it hit me. The lyrics to this song are based on Ecclesiastes 3:1-8. How I missed the obvious connection, I'll never know.

I've been thinking about that song a lot these days. Perhaps it was the shock of receiving my Medicare card in the mail. Maybe it was remembering the day that my brother looked at me and said, "Well, sis, I guess you're the family matriarch." It took me by surprise, but I quickly quipped, "Well, bro, if I'm the matriarch, you're the patriarch!" We both had a good laugh. If that wasn't enough, the family reunion reminded me that among the cousins on my mother's side of the family, I am the matriarch. Sobering realities. We may not like them, but they help us more than we know.

The seasons of life encircle us from first breath to last. The dash on our tombstones represents the seasons we encounter between the date of our birth and the date of our death. The dash represents the totality of all our days.
Each season is unique. Each is formed by our experiences and the choices that we make. Successful navigation through each of the seasons requires intentional, thoughtful living. More than ever before, today's complex world, with its unprecedented possibilities for connection through technology, requires that we be able to adapt to simultaneous realities.

2

Though complicated by this complexity, each season of life has both tremendous blessings and also specific issues, problems, and challenges. The sad truth is that more often than we'd like, we get out of sync with life. We hold on when we should let go. We let go when we should hold on. We speak when we should be quiet. We are quiet when we should speak. We try to recapture youth when youth is long past. We want to be adults before our time, without realizing what it means to be an adult. We fail to ask ourselves, "What time is it in my life? What do I need to do at this time in my life? What do I need to do to prepare for what comes next?" Failure to ask these questions, to come to terms with the ages and stages of our lives, is a sure path to unhappiness. Knowing what to expect at each stage can not only prepare us for the good in life, but it can also help us avoid many pitfalls.

Successful navigation of life's seasons requires continuous adaptation to changes, positive or negative, in our circumstances and environment. Sometimes these changes involve significant losses that alter the course of our lives. Without appropriate guidance and support, we are likely to adjust ineffectively and/or make decisions that have a negative impact not only on our lives, but also on the lives of others. Knowing what to expect prepares the way for better decision-making and better quality of life at each season.

3

Seasons of Life

One way to think about the seasons of life is to consider each decade as
illustrated below:

▶ Greening for Greatness
  ▶ Trying Twenties
    ▶ Terrific Thirties
      ▶ Fabulous Forties
        ▶ Fantastic Fifties
          ▶ Sensational Sixties
            ▶ Significant Seventies
              ▶ Effluent Eighties
                ▶ Naissant Nineties . . .
                and Beyond

Let us explore each season.

Greening for Greatness

The first period, age 0 – 20, covers the formative years of childhood, the teen years and early adulthood. These are the years when others care for us and teach us to care for ourselves. These years can be relatively care-free since adults are responsible for caring for children. Young people are considered "green" because, like a newly budding plant, there is so much to develop.

Childhood can be filled with many happy memories as parents (or other guardians) learn and grow with their children. The challenge for parents is to grow in parenting skills as the child grows in age. For example, treating teens with the same parenting skills that we used when the children were in toddler and elementary phases can cause major problems in the parent-child relationship.

Leaving children to fend for themselves is also problematic. If adults are neither mature nor responsible enough, childhood years can be difficult years. Woundedness at this stage can be especially damaging since young people may not have developed the skills or acquired the resources for dealing with the adversity that comes their way.

The transition to adulthood begins toward the end of this stage, generally somewhere between the ages of 17-20. By then, most young people have acquired a driver's license, a first car, held a part-time job, and begun dating. This is perhaps the age of the first serious girlfriend/boyfriend and the first heartbreak over a love gone wrong.

These are the years of beginning to establish an identity, of knowing what type of person we want to be and how we will earn a living. Generally, this period includes entrance into college, some other type of vocational training, or the military. This is a time of transition, a time of great vulnerability. Poor decisions at this stage can haunt us for years or, perhaps, for the rest of our lives.

The challenge for parents and guardians is to understand that not only has the world changed, it continues to change faster than it did when we were growing up. With each new generation, young people are exposed to more at an earlier age than their parents ever were. Consequently, young people need more resources, especially emotional and spiritual resources, than previous generations in order to deal with all the challenges that are part of their lives, from the temptations of drugs, alcohol and sex, to, perhaps more importantly, the complex ways that technology affects our lives and relationships.

Sadly, with church attendance increasingly on the backburner for many people and with churches reluctant to address critical issues, young people may grow up without lessons imparted from this important resource. Moreover, with computers, tablets, cell phones, texting, and all the rest, it is a challenge for parents to keep up, yet keep up we must. In spite of the competing demands of our busy lives, we must make our children a priority, not just with material provision, but with time.

The transition into adulthood will be smoother if young people do not have to fill in the gap or make up for essential life lessons and experiences that they did not get in their early years. With the right support, young people can thrive, flourish, and overcome even the worst circumstances. Despite the challenges, it is possible for young people to come to the end of these years, prepared for life and greened for greatness.

Trying Twenties

The Trying Twenties can be thought of as the season of "Welcome to the Real World," i.e. the real world of responsibility. This decade is the time of saying goodbye to years of preparation and entering the adulthood. It is a time of finishing college, joining the working world and the challenge of a first full-time job. The first job may include the shock of having a boss. It likely includes the shock of having a boss point out the need for improvement. This "need for improvement" can be bewildering for someone who sailed through the early years unscathed and untouched by the realities of life.

This is the time to contend with the reality of paying bills and what happens when bills aren't paid. A friend once told me of her daughter's surprise when she received her first utility bill. Accustomed to paying just her phone bill, her daughter inquired, "Mom, you mean I have to pay for water, gas, and electricity?" Children understand, perhaps for the first time, what a blessing it is to grow up in a home in which water and electricity flow without interruption.

If one gets married during this decade, this is the time of realizing that there's more—much more—to being married than being in love. This is the time of realizing that parenting is a 24 hours a day, 7 days a week job. Handling all of this can be a major shock if we are not prepared for the myriad responsibilities of young adulthood. College dreams may be deferred. A first job may come with unexpected pressures. There may be more "month than money," and marriage and family problems may emerge.

Good communication and problem-solving skills are the keys to successful navigation of these years. Planning ahead and dealing with problems as they arise, rather than denying or avoiding them has a positive effect on the quality of life. Problems denied, avoided, or handled poorly in this season will grow and resurface, demanding attention in later years. For example, a failure to establish good financial habits early in life will result in financial difficulties in later years. Failure to devote sufficient time, energy, and resources to marriage and family can result in dysfunctional family relationships, including divorce. Cultural messages and the media often overlook these realities. Unrealistic images that devalue life or convey a life of luxury and ease without consequences must be avoided.

The decade of the twenties is an age when it is easy to think we know everything, or at least everything we need to know about life. However, it is more likely that we know relatively little. If we have not already established the habit of seeking essential information before making decisions, this is a good time to learn to ask questions, read books, pray, meditate, and seek advice, as needed. With information at our fingertips, sometimes, even just looking something up on Google can be a good way to get needed information and advice. Approached with knowledge and wisdom, the twenties don't have to be trying. If we are responsible, they can, indeed, be thrilling!

Terrific Thirties

With the thirties, the rude awakening of "Welcome to the Real World" is long past. Yet, in many ways, life begins here. This is the age of, hopefully, having gained at least some wisdom for living. Young enough to have plenty of energy for living, yet old enough to have quelled the voices of craziness from the teens and twenties, this is an age for building a life and planning for the future.

This is the decade when we may have achieved a measure of personal success at work. Success, however, is likely to come in the midst of increasing stress and workplace demands. Continued progress may mean that a new job, perhaps requiring a move to another location, may be on the horizon. As exciting as starting a new job can be, it also brings with it renewed pressures to prove ourselves all over again.

If decisions about marriage have been delayed, there may be increased stability on which to begin marriage and family life. It may be a good time to pursue an advanced degree. The demands of work and school make it more difficult to meet the needs of home and family. Spouses need attention. Children have school commitments, extracurricular activities, and need help with homework. Family calendars leave little room for household chores and family time. Unless given priority, church is just another item on the "To Do" list. This item is often skipped or discarded altogether. Parents, married and single, may be too frazzled to keep everything going smoothly. Children may feel bewildered, insignificant, unimportant, and be left to fend for themselves.

Perhaps the biggest challenge is making it all run evenly, at work, at home, at school, at church, and in the community. Good time management is a key to keeping this phase of life balanced. Prioritizing is crucial for managing the competing demands of this season of life. Otherwise, there will be too many loose ends, too many balls dropped, too many needs unmet.

As necessary as it is, open communication is easier said than done. Good conflict management needs to be truthful, yet loving and respectful at all times. It is essential to maintaining good relationships, especially at home and at work. This skill is hard to come by, especially when dishonesty, disrespect, and a lack of civility are so prevalent in the public arena. Wounds from the past that remain unresolved may surface and make communication more difficult. Professional help may be needed if an individual or a couple is to move past a communication impasse.

With all these challenges, we are likely to wonder, "What's so terrific about the thirties?" The thirties are terrific because they are full of possibilities. With more years ahead than behind, possibilities for success in this season are limitless. Much of life is still a blank slate yet to be fulfilled. Choices made in this decade are likely to set the trajectory for years to come.

Fabulous Forties

Despite the cultivation years of the thirties, some say that "life begins at 40." This is not a new idea. Rather, it began with a popular book that was published during the Great Depression, Life Begins at 40 by Walter Pitkin. The book assured its readers that despite the difficulties of the times, life could still be wonderful.

The forties is the decade of having it all together, or at least most of it. It is the age of benefitting from the good decisions of the past and lessons learned along the way. Struggles of the younger years are past. Children are grown or at least, almost grown. Even though a family's financial obligations may include college expenses for children, parenting is less about doing for children and more about guiding them and giving them room to grow. Work, while still demanding, begins to come into its own.

With so many life issues either resolved, or at least managed effectively, this is likely to be an age of transition and discontent. Many hit the so-called "Mid-Life Crisis" and ask, "Is this all there is to life?" People going through this internal struggle find that good relationships and a good career are just not enough.

Abraham Maslow, a psychologist best known for categorizing and defining the human "hierarchy of needs," would likely say that this is the time when physiological, safety, belongingness and love, and esteem needs have all been met. This is the time when the need

11

for self-actualization, that is, self-fulfillment, becomes more prominent.

I think of this as the age of divine discontent. As unsettling as it might be, divine discontent is a blessing. Divine discontent is propelled by the knowledge, interests, skills, and abilities that we have acquired over the years which have not been fully expressed or developed. It is driven by a desire to share our gifts in new ways. It is a time for acknowledging life's many blessings and realizing that blessings come with the responsibility to share with others. Perhaps the greatest task of this period is figuring out how to share our blessings with others. We are reminded of that in Genesis 12:2 God told Abraham:

I will make of you a great nation, and I will bless you, and make your name
great, so that you will be a blessing. NRSV
Answers to the question, "Is this all there is?" often inspire us to change careers, go back to school, open a business, start a non-profit organization, or give back in other ways. This may be the time for pursuing dreams and visions that just would not die. Success in this season requires a willingness to follow our dreams. Answers can lead to a life that is more fulfilling than anything that we could have imagined. Is it any wonder that the 40's are fabulous?

Fantastic Fifties

Some say the fifties are time for the "Bucket List." However, bucket lists focus on what we want to do before we die. Personally, I would rather focus on what I want to do with my life. I prefer the idea of "Imagination List." Ephesians 3:20-21 reads:

Now to him who by the power at work within us is able to accomplish abundantly far more than all we can ask or imagine, to him be glory in the church and in Christ Jesus to all generations, forever and ever. Amen. NRSV

Years ago, long before bucket lists and based on this verse, I began an "Imagination List." I wrote down any and everything that I wanted to have happen in my life, no matter how far-fetched or impossible it seemed. It has been amazing to see many of those things become realities in my life.

For some, this is an age of continued reassessment, perhaps a resetting of the direction of our lives. Often this is the decade of early retirement. Perhaps, the biggest new challenge is caring for parents when they are not able to care for themselves. The sandwich generation often begins here when we are responsible for caring for both parents and children. Occasionally, grandparents find they are raising their grandchildren or parents find that adult children have returned to the home. The pressures of meeting the needs of different generations can be overwhelming. We need not think that we have to do it

13

all by ourselves. We should feel free to ask for help when we need it. Willingness not only to reassess the direction of our lives, but also to ask for help can make the fifties truly fantastic.

Sensational Sixties

This is an age when some say, "Life just gets better." Answers to divine discontent become clear. Health and wellness may become a priority. If we are in good health, this can be a very enjoyable time of life. Children have their own lives. Grandchildren and great grandchildren are likely to be the new pride and joy.

Family responsibilities may change, often due to the death of beloved parents. Recognition of our mortality and the desire to leave a legacy start to become important. Wisdom and integrity gained through encounters with everyday living are an integral part of our identity.

The need to feel that we have accomplished something important and/or made a difference in the lives of others increases as we enter this decade. Recognition that life is more than just a series of unrelated events, but that every moment has the potential to be meaningful begins to take hold.

Self-assessment and asking questions such as: "What have I given? What do I have yet to give?" come to the forefront. Many find that we have much to give and that this is a good time to embark on new endeavors. I know a woman who, in her sixties, opened a bookstore and eatery that flourished for years. Imagine that! What an inspiration!

While there may be some recognition of slowing down, for many this is a time of getting and giving the most out of life. Freedom from work and family responsibilities creates a space for doing what we really love. For some, this is the time of starting a second or third career. It is a time when disparate pieces gathered from the various seasons of our lives somehow come together and, perhaps for the first time, finally make sense. When the pieces make sense, the sixties are truly sensational.

Significant Seventies

Since people today live well into their eighties, the seventies are not what they used to be. Although clearly, we have fewer years ahead than behind, still these can be fruitful productive years. If not already retired, this may be the decade of retirement. The seventies are an age when we can enjoy a lifestyle without the demands and stress of the workplace. If work continues, it generally proceeds at a somewhat slower pace. We might engage in some form of self-employment. Volunteer work may take the place of regular employment. Volunteer work may provide an outlet not only for giving back to the community, but also for using gifts and pursuing interests that remain dormant.

This is a stage for truly knowing who we are. Not just in terms of relationships with others or work and accomplishment, but in terms of a well-established personal identity, undeterred by circumstances and situations. It is the era of having an unflinching approach to life, of knowing who we are and what we are about. This is the age of living grateful for what lies behind, yet hopeful in anticipation of what lies ahead. This is the age of living based on who we are, not on what has (or has not) happened to us.

This is no time for sitting around and letting the chips fall where they may. With advances in health and wellness, we can expect that these will be years of continued productivity. The key to being productive is to stay connected. Staying connected to friends, family, and community is essential to our happiness during these years. If work, paid or unpaid, is still part of our lives, positive work connections are also part of living healthy and whole at this stage of life. Since people are social beings, finding ways to satisfy our need for relationships can make the difference in whether these years are painful or joyful. Even with the health challenges that are part of growing older, staying connected to people can lessen the stress of health and other concerns.

This is an age when taking care of our health really pays off. Years of paying attention to the three basics: exercise, eat right, get enough rest, even if these routines are relatively new, pays big dividends. Health concerns may require more time and attention. Chronic conditions continue and new maladies may arise. An encounter with a major illness or injury may require a major adjustment in lifestyle.

Questions about end of life matters (having a will/trust, funeral arrangements, etc.) come into focus. Though many would avoid dealing with such issues, dealing with them can be a source of peace and contentment. Responsible adults are concerned with getting their lives and their finances in order. Paying attention to these matters simultaneously gets them off our minds and prepares younger generations for dealing with the possibility of the death of their parents. Although these issues need to be updated periodically, discussing and settling these matters can bring peace to a family. When handled properly, with past and future in proper perspective, the seventies can be truly significant.

18

Effluent Eighties

This is the age of being well seasoned. Life spills out, oozes, flows out of and comes forth from us. This is an age when we can be a true inspiration to those younger than ourselves. Good health can make the difference as to whether we enjoy or dread these years. This is a time to relish in having made it through the previous decades and still having much, especially wisdom, to give others. The dignity and confidence that comes with having made good decisions along the way and having lived well speaks for itself. Knowing that we have done our best in the midst of issues, problems, and challenges of life, in the midst of losses and changes that have come our way make the difference between regret and contentment.

This is a time for making peace with our lives, for incorporating all the good and bad, the ugly and indifferent, into a single seamless whole. An inability to be at peace may leave us feeling defeated and bitter about life. Even though we may be slowing down, it is still important to stay active. Letting life flow makes the eighties effluent.

Some of us know what we want to be doing in our nineties and beyond. I hope we all do! While we never know just how long we will live, life planning should include these years. Expectations can make a difference in the quality of life at any time, but especially during these years. Lack of expectations makes us more vulnerable to depression and despair. Having something to look forward to in these years sets the pace and the direction for life.

Although there may need to be significant adjustments due to physical health, it is still possible to thrive during these years. We may have survived long enough to see the death of many cherished family members and friends. Focusing on the inner life can bring a sense of peace and wholeness. This is the age when that which has been born has come full circle, budding, dawning, and awakening to life in all its fullness. The key to an abundant life in these years is to come to terms with all that has been, and yet, what is to come. This is the time to know that the nineties and beyond are noble and it is ok to rest and take our place in the sun.

A CLOSING WORD

It is said that a life well lived speaks for itself. It is not a perfect life. It is not a life without struggles or ups and downs. Each season, each stage of life carries its own blessings. When all is said and done, there is a mystery that cannot be explained. There are questions that will forever be unanswered. Much will yet remain unknown. In each season, intentionality makes life worth living. Knowing what to expect, what is required can make all the difference. May you be blessed by knowing what to expect and what is required.

If these words have been a blessing to you, I want to hear from you. Feel free to contact me on my web page where you will find a listing of the products and services that are available:

dralfiewines.com

Now and always, God's best to you!

www.ingramcontent.com/pod-product-compliance
Lightning Source LLC
Chambersburg PA
CBHW071812020426
42331CB00008B/2467